Listen · Read · Think
SCIENCE

Bird Watch

Terry Jennings

Teacher Created Resources

First published in the United States by
QEB Publishing, Inc.
23062 La Cadena Drive
Laguna Hills
CA 92653

This edition published by
Teacher Created Resources, Inc.
6421 Industry Way
Westminster, CA 92683

www.teachercreated.com

Library of Congress Control Number: 2005921256

ISBN 978-1-4206-8151-2

Written by Terry Jennings
Designed by Melissa Alaverdy
Editor Hannah Ray
Picture Researcher Nic Dean

Series Consultant Anne Faundez
Publisher Steve Evans
Creative Director Louise Morley
Editorial Manager Jean Coppendale

Printed and bound in China

Picture credits

Key: t = top, b = bottom, m = middle, l = left, r = right

Corbis/Ron Watts 4, /Darrell Gulin 7, 22bl, /Theo
Allofs 8, /Joe McDonald 9r,
/George D. Lepp 10, /Tim Davis 13b, /Dieter
Zingel/Frank Lane Agency 14, 19b,
/Giraud Philippe/Sygma 15r, /Jonathan Blair 16, 21b;
RSPB Images David Tipling 17;
Still Pictures/Schafer & Hill 6l, /Manfred Danegger
12, 20b, /Alan & Sandy Carey 15t, 22tl.

Contents

What is a bird?

Birds live almost everywhere in the world. They are the only animals that have feathers. A bird's feathers keep it warm in cold weather and dry in wet weather.

All birds have two legs and two wings, and most birds can fly.

Beaks

A bird's mouth is called a beak. Different birds have differently shaped beaks. Birds that eat seeds have strong, thick beaks. Birds that eat insects have thin, pointed beaks. Hunting birds, such as owls and eagles, have hooked beaks.

Ducks, geese, and swans use their flattened beaks to **sift** food from the water.

Can you guess what these birds eat by looking at their beaks?

Feet

Have you ever looked at a bird's feet?
Owls and eagles have large feet
with sharp **claws**. They use their
feet to grab onto their **prey**.

Woodpeckers have two toes that point forward and two toes that point backward. This helps them climb trees.

Ducks, geese, swans, gulls, and other sea birds have **webbed** feet, which makes them good swimmers.

Feathers

The colors of feathers tell us which bird they come from.

Some feathers are small and soft. These feathers are called down and they grow all over the bird's body. They help keep the bird warm and dry.

The bigger, stronger feathers grow on the bird's wings and tail. They help the bird fly.

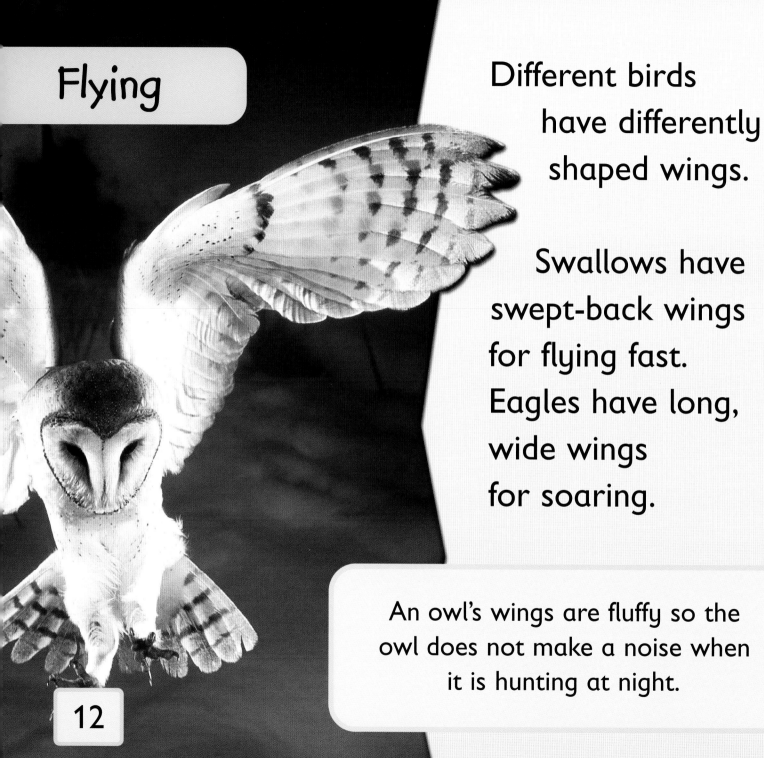

Flying

Different birds have differently shaped wings.

Swallows have swept-back wings for flying fast. Eagles have long, wide wings for soaring.

An owl's wings are fluffy so the owl does not make a noise when it is hunting at night.

Some birds can't fly. Penguins use their wings to swim fast through the water. Ostriches and emus can't fly either, but they can run fast.

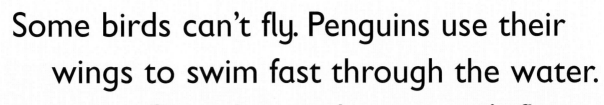

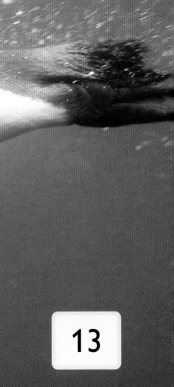

Birds lay eggs

Birds build their nests in the spring.
The mother bird lays eggs in the nest and
then sits on her eggs to keep them warm.

14

After two or three weeks, a baby bird **hatches** from each egg. Most baby birds are born blind and helpless. The mother and father birds feed the babies in the nest.

A few baby birds can run around and feed. They still need their mother to keep them warm and safe.

Birds in winter

Some birds fly to warmer areas for the winter. Swallows and some geese and gulls do this. In the spring, when it is warm again, these birds fly back.

Other birds come
near our homes
in winter.

We can feed
these birds by
putting out some
of the foods
that they like
to eat, such as
peanut butter
and bird seed.

Why does a bird need feathers?

Which part of a bird tells you what it eats?

18

Where do the birds with webbed feet live?

When do birds build a nest?

19

How long does it take for a bird's eggs to hatch?

Why do owls need to be able to fly quietly?

Name some birds that can't fly.

When do some birds fly to warmer areas?

claws—the hard, sharp nails on a bird's foot.

hatch—to break out of an egg.

prey—an animal that is hunted by another animal.

sift—to separate one thing from another.

webbed—joined together by flaps of skin.

22

Index

Parents' and teachers' notes

- Look through the book. Does your child know the names of any of the birds in the photographs?
- Observe birds in a yard, garden, park, or on school grounds. Look carefully at their beaks and feet and discuss how the birds use them.
- Explore moving like birds—running, hopping, standing on one leg, flapping wings (arms!).
- Make a list of "bird words" with your child. Encourage your child to draw a picture to accompany each word.
- Put out piles of different seeds and see which kinds of birds eat what. Give the birds a shallow dish of water and observe how they drink and bathe. (Keep all the food and water out of the way of cats!) Encourage your child to keep a diary of the birds that come to your feeding station.
- Make a collection of clean feathers. Mount them on paper or cardboard using tape. Always wash your hands thoroughly after handling feathers.
- Discuss how birds keep warm in cold weather and what we do to keep warm when the weather is cold.

- In the early spring, make a collection of old pieces of yarn (cut into short lengths), hay, feathers, pet hair, moss, and other soft materials. Put them all in a net bag. Hang the bag up outside, and watch to see which birds come and collect these nesting materials.
- Can your child remember which birds cannot fly? (For example, penguins and emus.) What are these birds good at doing instead?
- Talk about how different birds' wings, feet, and beaks have adapted to suit their different diets and habitats.
- Look through some other bird books with your child. How many birds' names can you find that include colors? Make a colorful poster featuring these birds.
- Does your child have a favorite bird? Using books and the Internet, help your child find out some facts about his or her chosen bird. Together, create a fact sheet about this bird. Include drawings of its feathers, feet, and beak.